HOLY SPIRIT POWER MINISTRY

By
Dorothy Agatha Lambie

Copyright © 2012 by Dorothy Agatha Lambie
Canadian Copyright © 2012

HOLY SPIRIT POWER MINISTRY
by Dorothy Agatha Lambie

Printed in the United States of America

ISBN 9781622309443

All rights reserved solely by the author. The author guarantees all contents are original and do not infringe upon the legal rights of any other person or work. No part of this book may be reproduced in any form without the permission of the author. The views expressed in this book are not necessarily those of the publisher.

Unless otherwise indicated, Bible quotations are taken from *The New King James Version*. Copyright © 1982 by Thomas Nelson;

www.xulonpress.com

Table of Contents

The Purpose Of This Book!!! vii

Acknowledgements!!! ix

Chapter One   Who Is The Holy Spirit? 11

Chapter Two   Why Was The Holy Spirit Given To The Christian Believer? 16

Chapter Three   What Should Be Our Responses To The Holy Spirit? Or How Should The Christian Believer Relate To Holy Spirit? 33

THE PURPOSE OF THIS BOOK!!!

The purpose of this book is to give Christian believers a clearer understanding of Holy Spirit. That is, Who He is, Why He is given to us, and how we should relate to Him.

I have included some practical examples from my personal life showing how I relate to Him as God.

I deliberately quoted some Scripture passages to illustrate the points. This is because of the varied versions of the Bible. Also I am well aware that some Christians do not take the time to read the Bible; and so they are not familiar with its contents.

My prayer is that after reading this book, the reader will find it spiritually enlightening, practical, and informative.

Finally, I hope everyone will develop a closer relationship with God as a result of reading this book.

ACKNOWLEDGEMENTS!!!

I would like to thank Holy Spirit for His Leadership, Guidance, Wisdom, Knowledge, and Understanding; as well as the practical Instructions that He gave me to enable me to write this book.

I would also like to thank the people who prayed for me and my ministry.

GLORY BE TO GOD THE FATHER,

GLORY BE TO GOD THE SON,

GLORY BE TO GOD THE HOLY SPIRIT.

AMEN!!!

"NOT BY MIGHT NOR BY POWER, BUT BY MY SPIRIT SAYS THE LORD OF HOSTS"
(Zechariah 4: 6).

Reverend Dorothy Agatha Lambie, B.A., M. D.I.V.
(Dorothy Agatha—- means; good gift of God in Greek. I hope and pray I will be able to live up to my name).

Chapter One

WHO IS THE HOLY SPIRIT?

The Holy Spirit is God. He is the third Person of the Holy Trinity.

He exists eternally. The Spirit of God was hovering over the face of the waters during creation. (Genesis 1:2)

> "For there are Three that bear witness in Heaven: the Father, the Word, and the Holy Spirit; and these Three are One" (1 John 5:7).

The Holy Spirit was given to the Christian believers as a group on the day of Pentecost. Prior to this event He was given to specific individuals as determined by God. Examples of these are David, Samson, Samuel, Nathan, Elijah and Elisha.

Since Pentecost whenever a sinner accepts Jesus Christ as Saviour the Holy Spirit comes to live in that person at the point of salvation. Jesus refers to the Holy Spirit as our Helper, Comforter, and the Spirit of Truth. The Holy Spirit is the Spirit of Christ or the Spirit of God.

The Holy Spirit is the One Who convicts us of sin. He draws us to God for salvation.

He is the One Who builds His church; that is the body of believers worldwide.

He will not force His will on us. He is gentle and speaks to us in a quiet voice.

He prompts us once or twice in accordance with the plans and purposes He has for our lives.

We should relate to Him in silence and / or solitude in order to hear Him. We cannot hear Him speaking to us in our thought processes if we are focusing on the television, internet or when we are talking on the cell phone. He reminds us of Scripture but we need to read the Bible first; or there will be nothing in our spiritual bank for Him to give us.

He is very patient with us. He is the Spirit of Christ in us. He does miraculous healings and many supernatural signs and wonders.

He is the Author of the Bible. He is the One Who inspired the various writers of the Bible.

This is the reason we ask Him for the interpretation when we need wisdom, knowledge and understanding during Bible studies.

He responds to faith in the believer. This is why as Christian believers we must always operate in faith. "Without Faith it is impossible to please God" (Hebrews 11: 6).

We pray to God the Father in the name of Jesus and God responds through His Spirit.

The Triune God work together always. They are three Persons but only One God.

We can address each One separately, however, the three Personalities are always privy to the conversation. God wants us to be open and honest in our conversations with Him.

God hates hypocritical behaviours and lifestyles. He also hates lukewarm Christianity.

> "And to the angel of the church of the Laodiceans write, "These things says the Amen, the Faithful and True Witness, the Beginning of the creation of God. I know your works, that you are neither cold nor hot.

I could wish that you were cold or hot. "So then because you are lukewarm, and neither cold nor hot, I will spew / vomit you out of My mouth. Because you say, "I am rich, have become wealthy, and have need of nothing and do not know that you are wretched, miserable, poor, blind and naked. I counsel you to buy gold refined in the fire, that you may be rich; and white garments, that you may be clothed, that the shame of your nakedness may not be revealed; and anoint your eyes with eye salve that you may see. "As many as I love, I rebuke and chasten. Therefore be zealous and repent" He who has an ear, let him hear what the Spirit says to the churches" (Revelation 3: 14-19, 22).

Strong words indeed. It sounds like a word not only for the Laodicean Church but for us in our twenty first century churches.

We are passionate about politics, sports, movies, Hollywood and other secular issues.

When we truly grasp Who God is; how can we be otherwise than excited and passionate about our relationship with Him. He is the greatest One in the entire Universe, and He wants to have a close, personal, intimate relationship with us mere human beings. He was willing to strip Himself of His Godly attributes for a season. He was willing to condescend to becoming a lowly human being in order for us to relate to Him, and to reconcile us to Himself. He was willing to be murdered for our sakes.

He makes Himself available to us twenty four hours a day. We do not need an appointment to connect with or talk to our heavenly Father. God is loving, kind, thoughtful, merciful, patient, forgiving and so wonderful in so many ways. Let us be anxious to talk to Him twenty four hours a day. We really lack wisdom when we neglect to take the time to talk to God. As Christians we have no excuse we are supposed to know what the Word of God states in the Bible. We are encouraged to ask God for wisdom, knowledge and understanding. Let us ask Holy Spirit for wisdom.

God is relational as is evidenced by the Holy Trinity. He wants to relate to us and for us to relate to Him.

> "The fear of the Lord is the beginning of wisdom. And the knowledge of the Holy One is understanding" (Proverbs 9:10).

The Holy Spirit gives us spiritual discernment. He explains His Word to us. He is Holy. He is God. He is our Teacher and Instructor.

As Christian believers we become One with God because of the Holy Spirit Who dwells in us. We are the Temple of the Holy Spirit. The Holy Spirit comes to us with power and authority.

Are you aware If you are alone and you need someone to agree with you in prayer, you can ask Holy Spirit to agree with you? He is on Earth with us and in us. God the Father, and God the Son, Jesus, are in Heaven.

> 'Now He Who establishes us with you in Christ and has anointed us is God. Who also has sealed us and given us the Spirit in our hearts as a guarantee" (2 Corinthians 1:21-22).

> "Again I say to you that if two of you agree on earth concerning anything that they ask, it will be done for them by My Father in heaven" (Matthew 18:19).

The Holy Spirit convicts the world of Sin, of Righteousness and of Judgment.

Of sin because the unbelievers in the world do not believe in Jesus; He will convict the world of righteousness, because Jesus after His resurrection went back to the Father in Heaven. This is why Jesus does not walk the earth anymore in human flesh. He will convict the world of judgment because the ruler of this world is judged (John 16: 8—10).

The Holy Spirit will return to heaven with the believers prior to the coming tribulation.

This is because the mystery of lawlessness is already at work in the world. However the Holy Spirit Who restrains will do so until He is taken out of the way that is when the rapture occurs, at least as I understand it (2 Thessalonians 2:7).

Chapter Two

WHY WAS THE HOLY SPIRIT GIVEN TO THE CHRISTIAN BELIEVER?

He is given to the Christian believer as a guarantee of our salvation.

The Holy Spirit was given to us to enable Jesus Christ to live His life in and through us.

He was given to equip us for works of service or ministry in the kingdom of God on planet Earth.

HE GIVES US SPIRITUAL GIFTS

He Is the One Who gives us Spiritual Gifts, and enables us to use our gifts.

> "There are diversities of gifts, but the same Spirit. There are differences of ministries but the same Lord. And there are diversities of activities, but it is the same God Who works all in all. But the manifestations of the Spirit is given to each one for the profit of all" (1 Corinthians 12: 4-7).

> "For to one is given the word of wisdom through the Spirit, to another the word of knowledge through the same Spirit. To

another faith by the same Spirit, to another gifts of healing, by the same Spirit, to another the working of miracles, to another prophecy, to another discerning of spirits, to another different kinds of tongues, to another the interpretation of tongues. But one and the same Spirit works all these things, distributing to each one individually as He wills" (1 Cor. 12: 8-11).

Also in another Scripture passage,

"And He Himself gave some to be apostles, some prophets, some evangelists, and some pastors and teachers. For the equipping of the saints for the work of ministry, for the edifying of the body of Christ" (Ephesians 4: 11-12).

Needless to say we were given these gifts and empowered to perform them by the indwelling Presence of the Holy Spirit. There is no way any Christian could live the Christian life and operate in the gifts of the Spirit without the enabling Power of God.

The gifts and calling of God are irrevocable, this means these gifts will not be taken away from us. We are expected to fulfill the calling and use our spiritual gifts to edify each other to the glory of God (Romans 11: 29).

For those involved in recruiting ministry workers!!!

I know from personal experience, recruiting ministry workers can be frustrating at times.

Here is how I usually accomplish this task. The following is the strategy I employ.

I was Sunday School Superintendent for a medium size Church for five years. Whenever I needed to recruit workers/ teachers to fill a position the first thing I do is pray. The reason for this is, God has gifted His children with a variety of spiritual gifts. These gifts are intended to build His kingdom here on Earth. Therefore, keeping this fact in mind; God is the best Person to ask for help. He already knows who is gifted for which tasks. So during my prayer time with God I remind Him about the need for workers. He usually brings the names of the people to my mind. I would then connect with the person or the people by telephone or in person. I would inform the person concerning the prayer session. I would say your name came up, and so I would like you to pray about it, and give me your response. In almost one hundred per cent of the cases I would receive a positive response from the person within a few days.

I had a unique experience a few years ago. A number of people volunteered to go and restart a Church. I was a fulltime Seminary student at the time as well as the Sunday School Superintendent, and a Sunday School teacher. I was losing eight people to this group. However, I needed twelve people to replace the eight people. This is because some of the people were involved in two and three ministries. I assessed the situation and realized getting the replacements on time could be a real problem. Also I had assignments for my courses that I needed to focus on. So I spoke to our Commander and Chief, the Lord Jesus and I said; Lord Jesus, please provide the twelve people I need because I have my school work and I really do not need any headache at this time.

Saints of God, the answer was immediate. Within a few days I contacted the twelve people He told me to ask and everyone answered in the affirmative. And to confirm that this was a divine intervention and answer to prayer; the twelve people already had Plan to Protect training. I only needed to do a brief orientation. It was the easiest ministry recruitment I was involved in.

One of the things we need to remember is this; God wants us to work with Him, not just for Him. Remember it is His Church, and He has promised to build His Church. He has everything under control. This is why the Scripture states. "In all your ways acknowledge Him and He will direct your paths" (Proverbs 3: 5). I am really excited about this incident.

HE IS OUR HEAVENLY HELPER

As our Heavenly Helper He helps us in every aspect of our lives. There is no limit to the help available to us through Holy Spirit. As God His power is infinite. He is able to help us in spiritual and non spiritual every day matters.

Here is a case in point!!!

On one occasion in early December I went out to my front porch to put up Christmas lights. Now the location is Canada so of course the weather was cold. My intention was to exchange the current light socket with another one that would accommodate the holiday lighting. The procedure required the loosening of a screw. However, as it turns out I could not loosen the screw. The thought came to me to ask one of my neighbors for help. Being the stubborn person I am, I rejected the thought and I said to myself, I will ask God for help; because nowhere in the Bible does it say to ask my neighbor for help. On the contrary there are many passages encouraging the Christian believer to ask God for help. I was also being independent, and did not want to admit to my neighbor that I could not loosen the screw. So I asked God for help. After trying for a few minutes to loosen the screw, I was unsuccessful. I was getting frustrated at this point. In addition to my frustration, my fingers were starting to turn blue from the cold weather. I decided to ask God for help a second time. Still the screw would not loosen. I started to go back into the house, and I said out loud, why do I even bother? here I am praying, are you telling me God cannot loosen a screw? At this point I felt a strong prompt to try again, so I climbed up onto the chair once again and touched the screw. This time the screw was so loose it fell to the ground and into the flower bed below. I did not need to unscrew it, I merely touched it and it fell to the ground. I retrieved the screw from the flower bed. I replaced the light socket as planned; and got my Christmas lights set up as planned. I believe this incident was an exercise in perseverance. In any case God loosened the screw just as I was about to give up. As Christian believers we have Someone we can ask for help every time we need it. Actually God is the best Person to ask for help. Why settle for the rest when you already have the Best? YES REALLY!!!

HE PRAYS FOR US: HE IS OUR INTERCESSOR!!!

He prays for us with groaning we are unable to utter at times.

> "Likewise the Spirit also helps in our weaknesses. For we do not know what we should pray for as we ought, but the Spirit Himself makes intercession for us with groaning which cannot be uttered."

"Now He Who searches the heart knows

what the mind of the Spirit is, because He makes intercession for the saints according to the will of God"

"And we know that all things work together for good to those who love God and to those who are the called according to His purpose" (Romans 8: 27-28).

HE LEADS US AS SONS AND DAUGHTERS OF GOD!!!

"For as many as are led by the Spirit of God, these are sons of God. But you received the Spirit of adoption by Whom we cry out Abba Father"

"The Spirit Himself bears witness with our spirit that we are children of God" (Romans 8: 14-16).

So the Holy Spirit leads us as sons and daughters of the Most High God. This is in the plan and purposes of God for our lives. Let us obey His commands on a daily basis. We are not left to figure out things, or to contemplate the issues of life on our own. We have Someone to lead and instruct us along the journey of life. Let us talk to Him and ask for His help.

He leads us into all truth, and teaches us all things. As Christian believers let us be led by the Spirit of God every day. Let us stay tuned in to Him at all times. Not only are we to stay tuned in to His voice. Let us listen to, and obey the promptings that He gives us.

HE COMFORTS US!!!

He comforts us when we need to be comforted.

> "Blessed be the God and Father of our Lord Jesus Christ, the father of mercies and God of all comfort. Who comforts us in all our tribulation, that we may be able to comfort those who are in any trouble, with the comfort with which we ourselves are comforted by God" (2 Cor. 1:3-4).

> "God is Spirit and those who worship Him must worship in spirit and truth"(John 4: 24).

> "And I will pray the Father, and He will give you another Helper, that He may abide with you forever"

HE IS OUR HELPER!!!

> "But the Helper, the Holy Spirit, Whom the Father will send in My name, He will teach you all things and bring to your remembrance all things that I said to you" (John 14: 16-17, 26).

The Holy Spirit brings things such as the Scriptures to our memory as we need it; so that we can apply the Word of God to our lives. As a matter of fact Holy Spirit is so gracious He will even remind us of other things if we ask Him.

Allow me to share this incident.

About four of us ladies decided to go shopping at one of

the major shopping malls in the area. We were shopping for clothes among other things. I had a bridal shower to attend the next day, and so I needed a card for the occasion. Before I left home I asked Holy Spirit to please remind me to buy the card at the mall. So as anyone can guess we shopped until we were tired and ready to go home. I completely forgot about the card. We were on the escalator going up to the second floor from the first floor to get to our car, when Holy Spirit reminded me about the card I needed to buy. I went into the nearest pharmacy. I saw the pharmacy in front of me as I stepped off the escalator. This store had a card section, I bought the card and thanked Holy Spirit for reminding me. Now He reminded me at the right time, because if the reminder came while I was trying on clothes, or was shopping in one of the stores for sure I would forget by the time I left the store. You see, God knows us women and our shopping habits. Remember, He is with us always. He goes shopping with us. I remember on one occasion I went shopping by myself for a dress. Every time I tried on a dress I would ask Jesus if He liked the dress. He would say no; until I tried on one and right away He said yes this is the one to buy. The dress is perfect for me. To this day every time I wear the dress I still get positive comments from people.

HE TEACHES US AND INSTRUCTS US!!!

"These things we also speak, not in words which man's wisdom teaches but which the Holy Spirit teaches, comparing spiritual things with spiritual. But the natural man does not receive the things of the Spirit of God, for they are foolishness to him; nor can he know them, because they are spiritually discerned. But he who is spiritual judges all things, yet he himself is rightly judged by no one. For who has known the mind of the Lord that he may instruct Him? But we have the mind of Christ," (1 Cor. 2:12-16).

No one knows the things of God except the Spirit of God. But as it is written

"Eye has not seen nor ear heard, nor have entered into the heart of man the things which God has prepared for those who love Him"

"I will instruct you and teach you in the way, you should go. I will guide you with My eyes" (Psalm 32:8).

The Holy Spirit knows everything; and so He is the One Who is able to give us the wisdom, knowledge, and understanding we need for every aspect of our lives. He knows the end result from the beginning, and is able to keep us on track in all of our endeavors. We can rely on Him to show us the path to take. He can tell us when to start a business or ministry and explain to us all of the detail pointers we need to keep in mind. We are truly blessed as Christian believers. We each have our own personal advisor twenty four hours a day. Because He does not make mistakes we never have to be concerned about making the wrong decision for the rest of our lives. Of course we need to consult with Him just as we would any other personal advisor. The wonderful thing is that we do not need any other advisor. He is the only One we will ever need in this life. He can advise us concerning our finances, health, diet, our relationships with other people, our ministries, our spiritual gifts, our jobs, our hopes, dreams and our wishes. Need I say more; He is Omniscient. He knows everything. He is also Omnipotent. He can do anything and everything. Our God is in total control. Did you ever stop to think how thoughtful our God is? How did He know we would need a Personal Helper twenty four hours a day? He knew this because He made us, and wired us to need and to depend on Himself. In our affluent society most of us have a doctor, a dentist, personal counselor, dietitian, banker, personal trainer, teacher and tutor. In some cases an hairdresser, and a personal chef to mention a few.

HE REVEALS THINGS TO US AS OUR COUNSELLOR AND ADVISOR!!!

"But God has revealed them to us through His Spirit. For the Spirit searches all things, yes, the deep things of God" (1 Cor. 2:9-10).

The Holy Spirit is in the business of teaching us and instructing us. He reveals things to us according to the plans and purposes of God for our individual lives. So you want to know more about the Bible, or about God? Holy Spirit can explain all to you. Of course our brains are finite so He cannot reveal everything to us; because there is no way we could understand it all. However, He will reveal as much to us as we are able to grasp.

I can recall in the past when I was decorating my house, I ask God to help me choose my décor. He did, there was one instance when I wanted to purchase a black and white microwave oven, but when I got to the store they only had one in the colour black. So I bought it, but my first preference was for a black and white one, because these were the two colours I was working with. When the microwave was delivered a few days later to my home; to my pleasant surprise the microwave that came in the package turned out to be black and white. I said thank You Lord Jesus because I knew He was the one Who caused the supplier to send the wrong one as per my order. However it was the one I desired. The stones in my aquarium was another miracle. I picked a one – of- a - kind blend of stones for my aquarium. When I brought it home to my surprise it exactly matched a Batik painting of some fishes that was already hanging on the wall above the aquarium. The mix of colours were exactly the same as the aquarium stones. The colours are royal blue, white, aqua and dark blue. I have visited the same aquarium store for many years to purchase products; and to date I have never seen the same colour mix of stones as the one that I have in my home. Only God could have orchestrated such a match. I had no such match in mind. I did not remember the Batik painting when I purchased the stones. I only knew I did not want bright coloured stones such as red or orange.

    The unbeliever / natural man does not receive the things of the Spirit of God. They are not tuned in because they do not have the right to use the Password, that is available to every believer at the point of salvation. Not only do we have access to the things of God; we have the mind of Christ. We can think and react like Christ would react because of the Presence of the Holy Spirit in us. Saints of God we are not left on our own we have all that we need pertaining to godliness. "His divine power has given to us all things that pertain to life and godliness, through the knowledge of Him Who called us by glory and virtue" (2 Peter 1: 3). The unbeliever is on a different wavelength. He is tuned in to a different channel. His natural inclination is to reject the things of God. This is the reason the Word states "Therefore if anyone is in Christ he or she is a new creation; old things are passed away; behold, all things have become new" (2 Corinthians 5: 17). This is why the real Christian no longer have a desire for the things of the flesh; but have an increasing desire to please God.

WE HAVE ACCESS TO THE FATHER!!!

"For through Him we both have access by one Spirit to the Father" (Ephesians 2: 18).

Have you tried accessing your e-mail without the correct password?

It is truly a frustrating exercise. We need the correct password every time to obtain access. Our password to God is Jesus Christ. This is the reason we pray in His name. No one can come to God except through Jesus. He is the One Who died for us and is now in Heaven making intercession for us.

"I AM The Way, The Truth, and The Life, no one comes to the Father except through Me" (John 14:6).

"Nor is there salvation in any other, for there is no other name under heaven given among men by which we must be saved" (Acts 4:12).

"Now therefore, you are no longer strangers and foreigners, but fellow citizens with the saints and members of the household of God" (Ephesians 2:19).

But he who is joined to the Lord is one spirit with Him" (1 Cor. 1:17).

Have you noticed how Scripture confirms Scripture repeatedly?

He gives us wisdom, knowledge, understanding, and spiritual discernment.

HE IS OUR CONSTANT COMPANION!!!

The Holy Spirit is given to the Christian believer to live in and with twenty four hours a day for the rest of his or her life. Do you realize as a Christian believer, you cannot take a bath or travel to a vacation destination without Holy Spirit.

WE ARE CHILDREN OF GOD!!!

"For as many as are led by the Spirit of God, these are sons of God. But you received the Spirit of Adoption by Whom we cry out Abba Father"

The Spirit Himself bears witness with our spirit that we are children of God.

So we can know for sure we are children of God (Romans 8:14-16).

Did you know if you meet someone, and the person is falsely claiming to be a Christian believer? The Holy Spirit will confirm to you in your spirit whether the person is truly a brother or sister in Christ. This is another reason we need to stay tuned in to God.

WE ARE CALLED, JUSTIFIED AND GLORIFIED!!!

"And we know that all things work together for good to those who love God, to those who are the called according to His purpose."

"For who He foreknew He also predestined to be conformed to the image of His Son, that He might be the firstborn among many brethren.

"Moreover whom He predestined those He also "Called", whom He Called, those He also "Justified" and whom He Justified these He also "Glorified" (Romans 8: 27-30).

Notice nothing happens by chance; it is in the plan and will of God. The Holy Spirit is given to us believers to ensure and confirm our calling, justification and glorification.

But we have the mind of Christ. What exactly does this mean? It means we can think the way Christ thinks. It means we can be focused on the things of God. We can think and act in accordance with the will, plan, and purposes of God. We are heavenly kingdom oriented. Our minds are transformed and renewed by reading the Word. We now have a heavenly perspective on life. We think and act according to the Word of God. We have a desire to read the Word of God and to act on it. We are more interested in pleasing God than we are in pleasing other people. YES REALLY!!!

It means we go to God for daily instructions concerning our lives. Our desire is to please God. To bring glory and honour to Him. We become less self centered in our dealings with others. We love the brethren and desire the best for them. We are no longer in competition with one another. We pray for one another and take care of one another. We have compassion and are not self centered anymore. We become ambassadors for the kingdom of God. We represent God in spirit and in truth. We are servant oriented. We are disciples of Jesus Christ. We witness to the unsaved in words and actions. We disciple others to the glory of God. We spend time in prayer and fasting just like Jesus did when He was on Earth. YES REALLY!!!

We are fellow citizens with the saints and members of the household of God. Citizens of a country have certain rights, and yes obligations and responsibilities. This is why we can be seated in heavenly places with Christ Jesus.

We can live in the heavenly or spiritual realm. We can

operate in the spirit realm. Why? because we are equipped spiritually to do this. We have the Spirit of God in us and with us. We are predestined to be conformed to the image of His Son. We have no choice but to be like Jesus Christ. The Holy Spirit will make sure we are conformed to Christ's image. This is why the Word states we have been sealed with a guarantee (2 Corinthians 1: 22).

For some of us He allows circumstances in our lives to ensure this. Because of our stubbornness, we make life unpleasant for ourselves at times. But for sure we will be conformed, sooner or later. Of course our citizenship in heaven also comes with many blessings and the favour of God. We have access to Heaven twenty four hours a day. We have power and authority in the name of Jesus. We are princes and princesses of the most High God and of the kingdom of Heaven which extends to Earth here and now. Simply put, we have heavenly connections. YES REALLY!!!

This is why the scripture informs us "But you are not in the flesh, but in the Spirit, if indeed the Spirit of God dwells in you. Now if anyone does not have the Spirit of Christ he is not His" (Romans 8:9).

WE HAVE BEEN GIVEN A UNIQUE PRIVELEGE!!!

Saints of God, know this, we are the only people on planet Earth with the Spirit of God inside us. He is the One Who sets us apart from unbelievers.

> "And if Christ is in you, the body is dead because of sin, but the Spirit is life because of righteousness." "But if the Spirit of Him Who raised Jesus from the dead dwells in you, He Who raised Jesus from the dead will give life to your mortal bodies through His Spirit Who dwells in you" (Romans 8: 9- 11).

We become one with Jesus Christ because of His Spirit in us.

> "I do not pray for these alone, but also for those who will believe in Me through their word; That they all may be one, as You Father are in Me and I in You; that they also may be one in Us, that the world may believe that You sent Me "(John 17: 19-21).

WE ARE SEALED AND GIVEN A GUARANTEE!!!

The Spirit of God seals us, "Having believed you were sealed with the Holy Spirit of promise" (Ephesians 1: 13).

We are the temple of the Holy Spirit. This is a privilege that comes with a responsibility for us to live a holy life and keep our bodies and our spirit pure.

The Word of God sanctifies us. We are clean through the word (John 14:3).

This is another reason we should read the Word. It was given to inform us of the Truth.

HE COMES WITH POWER AND AUTHORITY

> "But you shall receive power when the Holy Spirit has come upon you; and you shall be witnesses to Me, in Jerusalem, and to all Judea and Samaria and to the end of the Earth"(Acts 1:8).

The Greek word is dunamis, from which we get the word dynamite. Power in this context means capacity, to be capable of, can do, ability, and capability.

This is why we can agree with the apostle Paul in Philippians 4:13, "I can do all things through Christ Who strengthens me." Without Me you can do nothing is a statement Jesus makes in John 15:5.

The Holy Spirit equips us for the circumstances we will face in life. He is Sovereign. He works in and through us to accomplish the tasks we were created to fulfill.

> "For we are His workmanship created in Christ Jesus for good works, which God prepared beforehand that we should walk in them" (Ephesians 2:10).

WHAT SHOULD BE OUR RESPONSES TO THE HOLY SPIRIT? OR HOW SHOULD THE CHRISTIAN BELIEVER RELATE TO HOLY SPIRIT?

In this section I will be sharing some personal episodes concerning how I relate to God. I hope these episodes will help to clarify and give you a better understanding of how to relate to Holy Spirit.

LET US WORSHIP HIM!!!

Our first response should be to worship Him and welcome Him.

Let us be careful not to grieve or quench Him. Remember He is a Person with feelings.

Let us develop a relationship with Him.

Let us talk to Him throughout the day and ask for His help. Let us ask Him for wisdom and guidance for the tasks ahead.

Let us talk to Him and ask for His help, leadership and guidance. We can share our thoughts, hopes and dreams with Him. He already knows them but He can help us formulate our ideas.

Let us tell Him we are sorry when we ignore Him, or put Him on pause like we do our cell phones.

Let us talk to Him about everything. He is the friend

Who sticks closer than a brother (Proverbs 18: 24).

Let us share our failures, triumphs, hopes, joys and wishes with Him. He is our True Friend.

Why would God the Father or God our Saviour, give us His Holy Spirit if not to converse with Him? He wants us to develop a close, intimate, personal relationship with Him. Because a close relationship with the Spirit of God means a close relationship with the Trinity. Namely, God the Father, God the Son, and God the Holy Spirit.

> That they may be one as You Father are in Me and I in You, that they also may be one in the Trinity (John 17:21).
>
> "And the glory which You gave Me; I have given them, that they may be one just as We are One, I, in them, and You in Me that they may be made perfect in one, and that the world may know that You sent Me and have loved them as You have loved Me."

Remember Jesus was praying for us too. We were on His mind even then.

How wonderful is the love that the Father has bestowed on us. There is no way we could even start to imagine such a thing. For sure we do not deserve any of it. Thank You God.

Question

Do you realize that as Christian believers we spend more time with Holy Spirit than we spend with our earthly family members? Of course He is our heavenly family Member, and He has a closer relationship with us than our children or our spouses. He is in us.

HE IS OUR CLOSEST FAMILY MEMBER!!!

We are the temple of the Holy Spirit. Let us not take this privilege lightly. Let us keep this fact in mind moment by moment. If we do, we will not be inclined to sin. Our thoughts can line up with the Word of God. We can make our thoughts captive to the obedience of Christ. We can live our lives to honour God on a daily basis. It really grieves the Holy Spirit when we talk about Him as if He is not present. For example, when we get into conversation about the Word of God, or talk about the things of God and fail to acknowledge His presence. Instead of asking Him; we go to commentators or biblical books to try to find out the answer; when He could readily give us the right answer.

LET US BE CAREFUL NOT TO QUENCH OR GRIEVE THE HOLY SPIRIT

Check this!!!

I asked Holy Spirit, what is one thing that really grieves Him?

His answer is, He wants to be a part of our conversations when we have Bible studies and discussions. It grieves Him when we neglect to ask Him to explain His truths to us. Remember He is the Author of the Bible. Also He is the One Who leads us into all truth and gives us wisdom, knowledge and understanding. He is present with us twenty four hours a day and is our Heavenly Family Member. YES REALLY!!!

You know in my opinion only God could devise such a plan. He knows we need Him twenty four hours a day. After all He is the Friend Who sticks closer than a brother. Some of us do call on Him twenty four hours a day or so it seems.

Speaking for myself I need His presence twenty four hours a day to keep me straight.

I cannot imagine spending a moment away from Him. Unbelievers do not know what they are missing. It is time for us to tell them and not keep this great truth to ourselves any longer. Just think about this for a moment. The God Who created the entire Universe, and everything, and everyone in it has condescended to live His life with us, and in and through us. The One Who knows everything and has the answers and solution to every problem is with us.

Students did you know you can ask Him to help you with school assignments, or to help you to remember things you would normally forget?

Do you know He can make you ten times smarter than your peers; like He did for Daniel and the three other Hebrew children? (Daniel 1:20).

THIS ACCOUNT IS FOR YOU STUDENTS!!!

This is a recent incident. I graduated from Tyndale Seminary in May 2011. This happened during my last year at Seminary. I was working on an assignment. I was at the Library the day before and read an article briefly, but I did not make a note of the Biblical reference. So here I am working on the assignment after 11:00 p.m. on Saturday night. I wanted to use the information I read but did not know where to find the reference. I flipped through Chronicles and Kings for about twenty minutes. By this time it was 11:30 p.m. So I prayed and asked for help to find it. After a few minutes I got no response. So I was getting angry. I said out loud to myself here I am it is 11:30 p.m. on Saturday night. I am teaching Sunday School at 9:30 a.m. tomorrow. I need to go to my bed. I cannot believe God is not helping me. So I said out loud. Lord Jesus, I am disappointed in You. Holy Spirit, I am disappointed in You. I said here I am doing Your work,

What Should Be Our Responses To The Holy Spirit?

You both know exactly where to find the verse I am looking for; and yet I am not getting any help.

I was quiet for about a minute. I started to flip through the pages of the Bible one more time. Suddenly my eyes landed on the verse I was looking for. I found it. I let out a scream so loud. It is a wonder no one came to knock on my door. The next day I told the incident to the students in my Sunday School class. I told them to ask God for help with their assignments, and not to give up, but to persevere. You see we can be ourselves, we do not have to pretend with God. He knows our thoughts so we may as well say what we are thinking. YES REALLY!!!

GOD IS THE MOST EXCITING PERSON TO TALK TO IN THE UNIVERSE!!! HE IS OUR FRIEND AND CONSTANT COMPANION!!!

Do you realize you are never alone and do not need to be lonely ever?

Do you know that you could spend some exciting time just sitting and talking to God? You could ask God a lot of questions about creation and about the universe that no scientist have even thought of to date. Do you know that God will give you answers to your questions? Do you know that talking to God can be just like talking to a friend on the telephone? You cannot see Him but you can sense Him talking into your thought process. There are times when He will send you to a Scripture passage; and you can converse that way. However, there are times when you can just sit and talk to Him about life in general; and He will talk to you about whatever you want to talk about.

Why spend time watching television when you can sit and talk to God? I am not talking about praying to Him, or asking Him for things. I mean just to sit and talk to God, like you would sit and talk to your best friend. Indeed let Him become your best friend. He will not laugh at your crazy ideas, and He will not gossip to anyone about your silly ideas. In fact He will give you ideas to start a ministry or a business. For sure you will be successful at whatever you do; when you discuss your ideas with Him prior to implementation. Let us get into the habit of spending quality time talking to God. After all prayer is talking to God, and listening to Him. We spend hours on social networks, and neglect the only One Who is truly worth spending time with; and in conversation with. This is one reason for this statement "My people are destroyed for lack of knowledge" (Hosea 4: 6).

A few years ago I was sitting and talking to God. So I said to God, the quality I like and admire most about You, is Your thoughtfulness. I said I know most people talk about Your Faithfulness, and I admire this quality too. However, the thought comes before the action, so Your Thoughtfulness is more to be admired. Now a few seconds later, I was really bold and so I said to God. Is there any quality that you like about me? To my surprise, God answered and said, I really like your openness and honesty when you talk to Me. I like the fact that you get straight to the point. You do not try to pretend or beat around the bush. I was truly surprised, I did not expect to hear that answer.

HE IS OUR ALL SUFFICIENT GOD!!!

What a thoughtful God we worship and serve!!!
This may come as a shock to some of you but it is okay to talk frankly to God. He already knows what we are thinking. On another occasion I was just sitting in my kitchen and just sharing my thoughts with Him and I said to God. Do you know how You are always telling me to share my income tax refund with others. How come I seldom have anyone walking up to me and giving me money; or sharing their income tax refund with me? I am not rich, I certainly could

use some extra money at times. I was not really complaining, I was merely sharing my thoughts with God. So imagine my surprise when about three weeks later a couple came to visit me at my home and gave me a certified cheque for six thousand dollars ($ 6000: 00). The couple gave me the money to help with the finances for a special birthday party I was planning. I knew right away this was an act from God. It has not happened before nor since that time.

"He who has pity on the poor, lends to the Lord. And He will pay back what he has given." God will not be a debtor to anyone.

God is always listening to us and paying close attention to our comments. He does not ignore us. Being obedient helps in our relationship with Him. At the very least let us be ready to ask Him for forgiveness; and let us keep our hearts pure and free from bitterness. Let us stay tuned in, and keep our relationship with God current. In other words let us not ignore Him in the good times, and come running to Him when things are bad. He will still be willing to help us. But we will feel like real hypocrites, because our consciences will make us feel bad.

HE GIVES US STRENGTH!!!

Let us stop saying we are weak, because we have His strength if we have accepted Jesus as our Saviour and Lord.

> "I can do all things through Christ Who gives me strength" (Philippians 4:13).

Let us start reading the Word and become familiar with the Word so Holy Spirit can use the Word to equip us, and to encourage us. He says He loves being on earth in us and with us; even though we sometimes ignore Him, and forget Him in our conversations.

Thank You Holy Spirit for Your patience with us.

Saints of God, Holy Spirit is our Link to the heavenly realm.

> "Greater is He Who is in me, than he who is in the world" (1 John 4:4).

As Christian believers do we really understand what this verse means?

It is time for us to ask Holy Spirit to explain it to us.

Here is the explanation He gave me.

He is the all powerful, Omnipotent, all knowing, Omniscient, ever present, Omnipresent God.

WE HAVE POWER AND AUTHORITY IN THE NAME OF JESUS!!!

This means we have authority given to us by God to use the name of Jesus to do exploits on Earth and in the Universe on an ongoing basis. In Him we live and move and have our being. We can do the miracles Jesus did and more because we have His Spirit residing in us permanently. We have been empowered for this reason. I believe our biggest stumbling block is unbelief. Without Faith it is impossible to please God. We do not receive because we do not have the faith to ask; and to expect what we ask or say to happen.

Check out these words of Jesus, "Most assuredly, I say to you, he who believes in Me, the works that I do he will do also and greater works than these he will do, because I go to My Father, and whatever you ask in My name, that I will do, that the Father may be glorified in the Son, If you ask anything in My name I will do it" (John 14: 12-14). Are you convinced as yet?

What Should Be Our Responses To The Holy Spirit?

Check out this incident which took place on February 23rd 2012.

Environment Canada issued a forecast for up to twenty centimeters of snow for the Greater Toronto area. The forecast was for the snowfall to start on the Thursday night around midnight and to continue into Friday afternoon on February 24th 2012. There was no snow storm. Here is the story behind that story. Two and a half weeks prior to this date, my niece telephoned me and told me she was making plans to take her mother and myself, to the Soweto Gospel Concert, on Friday February 24th at the Sony Centre in downtown Toronto. This is an African Choir group on tour. My sister and I both celebrate birthdays in February. My birthday was on February 16th and my sister's birthday was on the 24th, the day of the concert. During the conversation my niece told me she would be driving in to work that day, instead of taking the Go Train into Toronto from Hamilton; as is her normal method to commute. I told her I would pray for good travelling and driving weather for that day. She later told me she would be taking us out to dinner prior to the concert. After talking with her I prayed and asked God to ensure there was no snow nor freezing rain on February 24th, so my niece can drive from Hamilton and so we can celebrate our birthdays as planned. So imagine my surprise when I heard a forecast on the 680 Radio station Wednesday February 22nd calling for a major snow storm in the Greater Toronto area. This was supposed to be the biggest snowfall for the winter season. Prior to this month the snow falls were 2 to 3 centimeters of snow. There was one day when there was 5 centimeters of snow. The snow plows have not been on the residential streets in the Greater Toronto Area all winter because of the low snow fall all winter. Family day was on the Monday, and the weather was mild and sunny, as was Tuesday, Wednesday, and Thursday. I normally fast on

Mondays but I spent Family day with relatives. So I decided to fast and pray later on during the week. I was fasting on Thursday the 23rd and I was determined that the enemy was not going to ruin our birthday celebration plans. During my prayer and fasting I reminded Jesus about the prayer request for good weather.

I said, Lord Jesus, You have to stop the snowstorm. I said, You cannot allow the Devil to win. I said, I asked you for good travel weather for that day more than two weeks ago; and even if I was asking You today for the first time; I would still expect You to act because You are God and nothing is impossible for You. I said, I asked You for a favor, and there is no way the enemy is going to just step in, and do what he wants. The Lord Jesus then spoke directly into my thought process and said. Listen, you do not have to ask Me to stop the snowstorm; you can stop it yourself. I said out loud, do You mean I have the authority to command Angels? He said yes, you have the authority. The Bible verse "Greater is He Who is in me than He who is in the world" popped into my mind. So I went to the window in my ensuite bathroom, I opened the window and I yelled out into the atmosphere three times; I rebuke you impending snowstorm in the name of Jesus Christ of Nazareth. I cut you off and command you to cease now, in the name of Jesus Christ of Nazareth. Holy Angels please go and dismantle the snow storm system. Greater is He Who is in me than he who is in the world. I then closed the window and went back to my bedroom. I said out loud the Devil is going to see who is in charge here today. I kept saying, greater is He Who is in me than he who is in the world. I also said no power on earth can cause a snow storm in this area today or tomorrow and no power in heaven will cause a snow storm to happen in Jesus' name. I said not on my watch. "—He Who is in you is greater than he who is in the world" (1 John 4: 4).

I was 100% sure by 7: 00 p.m. that evening there would

be no snowstorm. As a matter of fact I asked God if I should e- mail or telephone Environment Canada to inform them the snowstorm was cancelled. He told me if I did they would not believe me so I should not inform them. Of course there was no snowstorm Thursday or Friday February 24th, 2012.

I was truly tempted the Friday morning to contact Environment Canada. They said they did not know why there was no snowstorm. We went out for dinner and to the concert as planned, and we had perfect driving weather going and coming back home that night. My niece drove in to Toronto in perfect driving conditions that morning.

THANKS BE TO GOD WHO ALWAYS GIVE US THE VICTORY IN CHRIST JESUS.
Talk about power and authority!!!

My sister and I are prayer warriors, and so we are a threat to the kingdom of darkness. I was sure this sudden forecast for a major snow storm was a plan of the enemy to get back at us. Of course the next day Environment Canada was at a loss to explain why the major snowfall did not happen. But I know I was the one God used to give the order to stop it. Every born again believer in Jesus Christ has the power and authority to do the same if we believe the word of God. I think the major reason we do not report more exploits like this is unbelief.

GOD THE FATHER IS VERY THOUGHTFUL, KIND AND LOVING!!!

On another occasion I asked God the Father for a specific request. After a few days I still did not receive an answer from Him. So I decided to go and reason with Him. I remembered the verse in Isaiah "Come let us reason together— —-

GOD ENCOURAGES US TO COME AND PRESENT OUR CASES TO HIM!!!

"Present your case, says the Lord. Bring forth your strong reasons." (Isaiah 41:21) and if this verse was not enough. Here is another,

"Put me in remembrance; Let us contend together; State your case, that you may be acquitted/ justified" (Isaiah 43: 26). I do not know about you, but this is an offer I could not refuse; so I decided to try it out and it worked. "For You have magnified Your Word above all Your name" (Psalm 138: 2). God keeps His Word.

Here is how I reasoned with my Heavenly Father on this occasion. I said to Him, Father God if I were You, and You were me, and You ask me for the request that I asked You for, I would grant the request. I then proceeded to explain the reasons why my request was reasonable for Him to grant. After listening to my explanation, God said to me you are right I will grant the request and He granted my request. The point I am trying to make is that when we remind God concerning His written word; He will be willing to discuss the issue with us. God is truly understanding, and delights in talking with His beloved children. God is a personal God. We do need to have reverential fear of God. However, we do not need to be afraid of God. We can talk to God about everything; this is the reason He makes Himself available to us twenty four hours a day. We are heirs to the throne of grace. As Christian believers we are sons and daughters of God, and as such we have special privileges. We are no longer strangers or aliens. The unbeliever does not have these privileges until when and if, he or she accepts Jesus as Saviour and Lord.

WE BELONG, AND ARE ACCEPTED IN THE BELOVED.   YES REALLY!!!

HE IS OUR INSTRUCTOR, HE CONVICTS OF SIN; AND HE IS OUR COUNSELLOR!!!

Here is an illustration to explain what I mean.

I was looking for a set of keys that I usually keep in one of the drawers in my kitchen.

After searching the drawers in the kitchen; I decided to ask God for help in finding my keys. By the way let God be your first aid; rather than your last resort. I am learning to ask God for help sooner than later.

After waiting a few minutes for Him to answer, I notice there was no response from Him.

Normally when I ask God for help He responds by talking directly into my thought process. In other words the answer comes to my mind.

After repeating the request out loud and still no answer; I asked God why He was not responding to my request? He told me, He was refusing to answer my request, because I had bitterness in my heart toward someone. I said really, who do I have bitterness toward? He said, do you remember three days ago you complained to Me and asked Me to tell another Christian believer to leave you alone; and to stop bugging you? I said yes, I remember. He said, you need to forgive the person. So I prayed right then, to forgive the person, and I asked God to forgive me. As soon as I finished praying, the thought came to me; go and check your jewelry box in the room upstairs. I went and checked the jewelry box upstairs and sure enough the set of keys was there. I have no idea how the keys got there. I thanked God for His help. This incident also reminded me that if we have unforgiveness or unconfessed sin in our hearts God will not hear us. "If I regard iniquity in my heart, the Lord will not hear me" (Psalm 66: 18).

When was the last time you asked God to help you in your every day affairs?

GOD GIVES US THE DESIRES OF OUR HEARTS; PSALM 37: 4

Sitting in my kitchen one evening after eating my dinner, I was just sharing my thoughts with Jesus. I told Him I was planning to take a trip overseas in a few weeks, but I wish I had about $ 1500 (fifteen hundred dollars) extra. The reason is, this was the amount it would cost me to do the things I wanted. I had picked up the mail on my way home from work, but I did not open the letters as yet. I was just talking to Jesus as I would talk to a best friend, just sharing my thoughts. I did not ask Him to help me. I then decided to open my mail expecting the usual bills. To my surprise there was a letter from my bank telling me they had deducted too much money toward my property tax and they were returning $ 1500 to my account. I almost fell off my chair. The bank normally pay my property tax for me. I said Lord Jesus, You knew about the letter all the time that I was sharing my heart's desire with You. Thank You. This incident happened a few years ago and has not happened since. But I will never forget it.

HE IS OUR GUIDE!!!

LET US ASK GOD FOR HIS SOLUTIONS INSTEAD OF GIVING HIM SUGGESTIONS!!!

It is a good idea to ask God for His solution, rather than tell Him what we want.

The following account will explain what I mean.

Several years ago someone gave me a huge flower pot.

What Should Be Our Responses To The Holy Spirit?

It is the type that people normally display on a front porch. I usually place the pot on my front porch every year. It has a Spider plant in it, and I usually add a couple of Petunia plants to it. The challenge for me, is getting the pot to the front of my home from the kitchen. So every year for about seven years I normally pray, and ask God to send me angelic help to lift up the flower pot with the Spider plant, and take it out to the front porch. The kitchen is at the rear of the house. Two years ago I asked God if He had a better solution. He told me to place the flower pot on a small area rug, and drag the rug with the flower pot to the front of the house. I did as I was told. I was truly surprised to discover how easy, and how simple was this idea. So I said Lord Jesus, You mean to tell me all these years I have been lifting the flower pot, and You did not suggest this idea to me. His answer is that I did not ask for His solution. He said, I asked Him to send me Angelic help and that is what He has been doing all these years. I could hardly believe it. The flower pot would remain on the porch from Spring until the Fall, that is from May until late September. I would normally lift it twice, once from the kitchen to the porch, and from the porch back to the kitchen. I certainly learned a valuable lesson that day, that I will never forget. God knows best; and He always has a better solution, than anything I can come up with.

GOD IS A PERSONAL GOD!!!

By now I hope you are getting the idea that the God of the Bible is a personal God and we can relate to Him. He is not a stone or wooden god. He is alive and responsive to us twenty four hours a day. WHAT A PLAN!!! THINK ABOUT IT!!!

Would you like to read something funny?

During my studies at Seminary I was required to take courses in both Hebrew and Greek, because my major was

Biblical Studies. I usually use a magnifying glass in my Hebrew classes; because of the fine print of the Hebrew Bible. On one occasion when I was using the magnifying glass to read, I spoke to Lord Jesus and said I should have taken these courses when I was much younger; this is ridiculous. I am the only student in the class using a magnifying glass. Without missing a beat, He said to me, well I did call you to be a Pastor twelve years earlier. Of course I could not say a word, because it was true. So I just laughed. Disobedience does have consequences. It took me twelve years to get serious, and answer the call to be a Pastor. I had perfect eyesight twelve years ago.

Now for those of you who think the snowstorm incident I mentioned earlier is just another isolated incident.

Here is another snow storm account for you!!!

On this occasion the snowstorm was already in progress. There was already at least two centimeters of snow on the ground.

Environment Canada forecasted a snow storm for the following day. It was supposed to start in the morning. I woke up at 5 a.m. the morning of the storm and looked out my window to see if the snow had started. My plan was to leave my car at home, and take the bus. But since the snow had not started as yet; I decided I would take my car to work. If I had taken the bus I would leave home at 6 a.m. I was going through the front door at around 7 a.m., when I noticed not only had the snow started, but it was snowing heavily.

I got into my car and drove off. By the time I got to Huntingwood and Brimley road, the route I normally take, there was a lot of snow on the road and the snow was still falling heavily. I was starting to regret not taking the bus. I was waiting to make a left turn at the traffic light. I then said out loud, Lord Jesus, You don't really expect me to drive all the way to work in this snowstorm do You? I said this, because I do not like to drive in snow. So this was my way to ask for help, from the One in control of everything. I said, how about stopping it. The Lord Jesus said to me, why don't you stop it. I said who me? You must be joking. He said, you can do it. You know what to do, I will teach you. So I rolled down the window on the driver's side and I said out loud. Clouds reconfigure; and stop snowing in the name of Jesus. To my pleasant surprise the snow stopped. By the time I reached Brimley and Sheppard, two blocks away there was no more snow flakes. I thanked the Lord for His help. This is the reason I was not surprised when He told me I could stop the snowfall myself on February 23rd 2012. I remembered this other incident. I was so surprised I did not record the date of this incident. This is because like you, I thought this was a one time isolated incident that happened years ago. Later on that evening, I heard the weather forecaster saying on the Radio he had no idea why the snow did not fall for a longer period of time; or why there was not more snow on the ground as per the forecast the night before. I thought it was an isolated incident, never to be repeated. But now I know better. PRAISE GOD!!!

HE GIVES US PROTECTION!!!

Here is another incident!

My job required me to attend a meeting in Mississauga on a specific day. I normally work downtown. I seldom use the highway because it is out of my way to get to work.

On this day I drove on the 407 Highway to Mississauga for the meeting. This happens to be my favorite highway route. After the meeting I got in my car to drive home. As usual I prayed for safe travel. I specifically asked God to give me angelic escort to travel home. By the way, this is one of our privileges as children of God. It was raining on the way home. I got into the centre lane on the 407 Highway going East and decided I would stay in this lane until I was ready to exit the Highway. About half way on my journey, I noticed a tractor trailer approaching in the centre lane, behind me in the distance. I said to myself, he sees me in this lane, and so he has plenty of time to change lane. I was here before him; and so I am not changing lane. As it turns out I was driving a little white Suzuki Swift car at the time. Instead of changing lanes, the driver came right up to within one car length of my car; and I guess he thought he would try to intimidate me in my little Suzuki. He travelled close behind me for about ten minutes. As a matter of fact, he was so close behind me, even if I wanted to change lanes I would not be able to do so safely; because I was unable to see into the other lanes on both sides of my car. Realizing he was trying to intimidate me; I started to say out loud this tractor trailer driver seems to think he and the Devil are in charge. He is certainly going to see that God is in charge. I also said out loud a few times. I come against you trailer driver with the Blood of Jesus Christ. There was no change, then I got the prompt, do not argue with him; just give the command. So I said out loud, I command you tractor trailer driver to change lane now, in the name of Jesus. While I was still talking he was changing lane. I would like to say I was not afraid during this incident, because I knew I had the Angelic escort I requested before I left the parking lot. I knew I was protected, and so the trailer driver could not touch my car. I knew I was safe. I am sure he will think twice before trying to intimidate another woman driver in a small car in the future. Of course I am not just a regular woman driver; I am one who knows I have heavenly connections. Let us expect God to answer when we pray. "Before they call I will answer and while they are still speaking I will hear " (Isaiah 65: 24).

What Should Be Our Responses To The Holy Spirit?

PRAISE GOD!!! PRAISE GOD!!! PRAISE GOD!!!

As you may have noticed, I am sharing some varied accounts to get you to realize God can, and will help us regardless of the situation we are facing.

Check out this incident!!!

Gardening is one of my hobbies. On this particular day I was doing gardening in my backyard. I was planting some flowering plants, and I needed about forty minutes more to complete the job. There was rain in the forecast for that day. Raindrops started to fall. I was not ready to stop gardening at this point in time. So I said out loud, Rain stop falling, wait until I complete my gardening. Come back in about thirty minutes. The rain drops stopped falling. I continued to do my gardening. I forgot about the rain. I was just about finished, when a sudden down pour of rain started. I had to run into the house to avoid getting soaking wet. I have to admit I did not expect the rain to stop. I was joking when I told the rain to stop. I did not use the name of Jesus or ask for heavenly assistance.

I thought about this incident for awhile and the only explanation that came to me is this-God spoke the world into existence and so since we have the Spirit of God in us as Christian believers, the elements are subject to us, and therefore respond to what we say. This is why we need to be very careful what we say, because our words are powerful. This is true of human beings in general; but even more so for us as Christian believers.

I do not know about you, but I am having an exciting time as a child of the Most High God.

Start asking Holy Spirit to explain His Word to you when you read the Bible. Let us start acting on the Word there are many pleasant surprises ahead.

I could share many more incidents involving myself and other people I asked God to help.

Let us remember to always give thanks to God for His help.

Let God know you love and appreciate Him.

If you are reading this book and you have not accepted Jesus as Saviour and Lord. The following is what you need to do:

A- Admit you are a sinner, because you are,
"For all have sinned and fall short of the glory of God" (Romans 3: 23).
B- Believe that Jesus is God, because He is God, and the only way you can be saved. He died to reconcile you to God, "if you confess your sins He is faithful and Just to forgive your sins and to cleanse you from all unrighteousness" (1 John 1:9).
C- Confess your sins to God and make a commitment to follow Him.

You need to be serious in this decision and after repenting, turn from your sins.

The Holy Spirit is given to the Christian believer at the point of salvation. He will help you to become a true disciple of Jesus. After making this decision you need to start reading your Bible on a daily basis and to start attending a Bible believing Church. One that teaches and preaches the Word of God without compromise. You will find you have a desire to read the Word of God, and to develop a relationship with God. You will also want to tell others about your new faith in God. You will want to pray to God, and to have fellowship with Christian believers. You will receive at least one spiritual gift and will have a desire to do ministry for God in accordance with the gift or gifts you have received.

May God bless you as you serve Him.

Lightning Source UK Ltd.
Milton Keynes UK
UKHW010144310821
389755UK00001B/11